# Today's Superstars
## Entertainment

# Adam Sandler

by Geoffrey M. Horn

GARETH STEVENS
GS
PUBLISHING
A Member of the WRC Media Family of Companies

Please visit our web site at: www.garethstevens.com
For a free color catalog describing Gareth Stevens Publishing's
list of high-quality books and multimedia programs, call
1-800-542-2595 (USA) or 1-800-387-3178 (Canada).
Gareth Stevens Publishing's fax: (414) 332-3567.

Library of Congress Cataloging-in-Publication Data

Horn, Geoffrey M.
     Adam Sandler / by Geoffrey M. Horn.
         p. cm. — (Today's superstars. Entertainment)
     Includes bibliographical references and index.
     ISBN 0-8368-4234-0 (lib. bdg.)
     1. Sandler, Adam—Juvenile literature.   2. Actors—United States—
Biography—Juvenile literature.   I. Title.
     PN2287.S275H67   2005
     791.4302'8'092—dc22
     [B]                                                    2005046503

This edition first published in 2006 by
**Gareth Stevens Publishing**
A Member of the WRC Media Family of Companies
330 West Olive Street, Suite 100
Milwaukee, WI  53212  USA

This edition copyright © 2006 by Gareth Stevens, Inc.

Editor:  Jim Mezzanotte
Art direction and design:  Tammy West
Picture research:  Diane Laska-Swanke

Photo credits:  Cover, p. 26 © Frank Micelotta/Getty Images; pp. 5, 8, 15, 20, 22
Photofest; p. 7 © Joseph Lederer/Fotos International/Courtesy of Getty Images;
pp. 11, 16, 18 © NBC. Courtesy: Everett Collection, Inc.; p. 12 © Kevin Winter/
Getty Images; pp. 24, 28 © Nick Gossen/AdamSandler.com/Getty Images

Printed in the United States of America

1 2 3 4 5 6 7 8 9 08 07 06 05

# Contents

# Chapter 1

## Laughing 'til It Hurts

What's the most embarrassing thing that happened to you today? Did you get a stain on your shirt? Spill some soup in your lap? Laugh so hard that soda came out of your nose?

It could be worse — a lot worse. You could be Bobby Boucher (boo-SHAY) in the movie *The Waterboy*. Adam Sandler plays Bobby. Bobby is a grown man, but he talks like a child. In one scene, Bobby invites his girlfriend Vicki home to meet his mother. Bobby loves Mama, and she loves him. But she doesn't want to share him with any other woman.

As they eat dinner, Mama tells Vicki about Bobby's bad habits. "Well," Mama says, "did he tell you about how much his feet smell?"

## Mama Had Doubts

Kathy Bates plays Mama in *The Waterboy*. Bates is a serious actress. She had doubts about starring in a comedy with Adam Sandler.

"I didn't know much about Adam Sandler," she told a reporter. "But my niece said, 'He's fabulous. You have to do this.'" She decided to do the film after she picked up the script and began laughing like crazy. "I ended up having a blast," she said.

In *The Waterboy*, Bobby Boucher gets dumped on at first, but he later becomes a football hero.

5

Vicki is not turned off. "Men are supposed to have stinky feet," she says.

"And are men supposed to wear pajamas featuring a cartoon character named Deputy Dawg?" Mama asks.

Vicki refuses to give up. "I happen to find Deputy Dawg very ... very ... sexy," she purrs.

Now Mama drops the bomb. She glares at Vicki and says, "Did he tell you about a little bedtime problem?" The screen shows a bed sheet with huge yellow stains. The audience howls with laughter. This whole scene is very funny — and very painful.

That's the key to a lot of Adam's humor. He makes embarrassing moments funny. You laugh at things that would make you cry if they happened to you.

## Fact File

The Waterboy was a big success. It cost about $23 million to make. But it took in more than $160 million in U.S. theaters alone.

**Adam's Inner Child**

In his movies, Adam often plays people who seem more like kids than grown-ups. They have a hard time controlling themselves. They get into mischief. They act out their anger with their fists. Sometimes, they talk in an odd way. They get teased. They are often underestimated — by parents, by rivals, and by bullies.

Adam often plays weird characters like Bobby Boucher. But deep down, they're good-hearted and well-meaning.

Adam plays a golfer with an anger problem in *Happy Gilmore*. Here he gets into a fight with game-show host Bob Barker.

## Mixed Reviews

Movie critics will probably never agree about Adam Sandler. Here's what one critic said about his movie *50 First Dates*: "Even by the standards of an Adam Sandler film, *50 First Dates* feels like a heap of recycled garbage." In a review of the same movie, a writer for *Salon* magazine sang a very different tune. "'Sexy' isn't a word that's often applied to Sandler.... But with *50 First Dates*, I think it's finally safe to consider him a sex symbol. He can ease a woman into a happy, confident state by reassuring her — with truth, not lies — that everything's going to be all right."

A childlike Sandler goes back to grade school in *Billy Madison*.

Here is another key to Adam's comedy. In the battle between the nice guys and the bullies, the nice guys come out ahead. They win because they learn when to fight and when not to fight. They win because they learn self-control.

Adam has been making people laugh for many years. He first became famous as one of the "Not Ready for Prime Time Players" on TV's *Saturday Night Live*. Today, he's one of the richest stars in the movie business. For a long time, movie critics said some very harsh things about him. They didn't like his childlike characters. They didn't enjoy his crude, gross-out jokes. In the last few years, however, even some of his harshest critics have started to come around.

As for Adam, he says he doesn't worry too much about the critics. "I really don't pay attention to what the world says about my movies," he told *E! Online*. "I just care about what my buddies think."

## Fact File

In *The Waterboy*, Bobby changes from dumped-on water carrier to football hero. Henry Winkler co-stars in the film as his football coach. Henry played Fonzie in the popular TV series *Happy Days*.

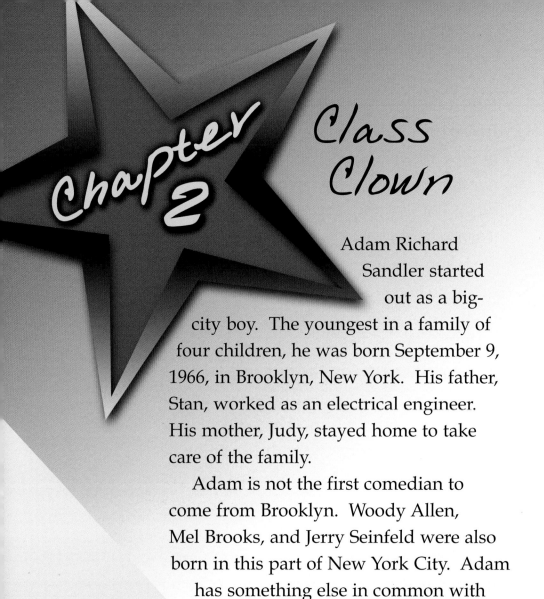

# Chapter 2

# Class Clown

Adam Richard Sandler started out as a big-city boy. The youngest in a family of four children, he was born September 9, 1966, in Brooklyn, New York. His father, Stan, worked as an electrical engineer. His mother, Judy, stayed home to take care of the family.

Adam is not the first comedian to come from Brooklyn. Woody Allen, Mel Brooks, and Jerry Seinfeld were also born in this part of New York City. Adam has something else in common with these famous comics. Like them, he is Jewish.

More Jews live in Brooklyn than almost anywhere else in the United States. During the

## Fact File

Adam used his parents' names in the title of one of his comedy albums. He called the CD *Stan and Judy's Kid*.

## The Hanukkah Song

"The Hanukkah Song" is one of Adam's most popular pieces.
It usually starts something like this:

> *Put on your yarmulke (YAH-mi-kah), here comes Hanukkah.*
> *It's so much fun-akkah to celebrate Hanukkah.*
> *Hanukkah is the Festival of Lights,*
> *Instead of one day of presents,*
> *We have eight crazy nights.*

**"The Hanukkah Song" became a yearly favorite on *Saturday Night Live*.**

## Carry a Big Shtick!

When Adam was growing up, his favorite comedy movie was *Caddyshack*. The film starred Rodney Dangerfield. He used to get laughs by saying "I don't get no respect." Dangerfield told stories about how his parents wanted to get rid of him. "I was an ugly kid," he said. "My mother had morning sickness *after* I was born."

Even after Dangerfield became a big success, he kept telling jokes about how everyone dissed him. People in show business call this kind of comedy "doing shtick." *Shtick* is a Yiddish word that means "piece" and also "prank." Comics who do shtick make people laugh by repeating the same basic gags and gimmicks.

Adam shared a laugh with Rodney Dangerfield at the Comedy Central awards show in 2003.

holiday season, people in some parts of Brooklyn are more likely to wish each other "Happy Hanukkah" than "Merry Christmas."

## New Kid in Town

In 1972, Adam's father took a job in Manchester, New Hampshire. It is about 250 miles (400 kilometers) from Brooklyn. The distance between the two places is not huge. But they are worlds apart.

When the Sandlers moved out of New York, they left one of the world's biggest cities. Now they lived in a small house in an old factory town. Manchester had some Jews, but not nearly as many as Brooklyn. Some kids in Adam's grade school teased him because he was different. "Everywhere I went, I heard comments about being Jewish, and it would hurt," he said later.

Adam wanted to be popular. He formed a rock band. He wrestled. He played basketball. But most of all, he became a class clown. Like many young comics, he learned a surefire way to become popular — get people to laugh with you, not at you.

## Fact File

Adam loves hoops. During the pro basketball season, he's often seen at Los Angeles Lakers games.

# Chapter 3 — Ready for Prime Time

When Adam finished high school, his choices were limited. "What do I want to do?" he would say to his brother Scott. "I don't like anything. I'm not good at anything."

Scott knew that it wasn't really true. Adam was very good at something — making people laugh. Scott urged him to try making a living as a comic.

One night, Scott took him to Stitches, a comedy club in Boston. By luck, it was open-mike night. Adam got up and began telling jokes. He was terrible. But he knew comedy was what he wanted to do with his life.

In 1984, Adam moved back to New York City.

## Fact File

Tim Herlihy was Adam's roommate at New York University. Later, he became Adam's writing partner on *Saturday Night Live*. Herlihy and Sandler have written many of Adam's hit movies.

## Comic with a Guitar

Adam used to get nervous in front of a crowd. He would panic and begin to stutter. His brother Scott suggested that maybe he would feel less nervous if he started out with a song or two. The idea worked. Adam began playing guitar and singing comic songs as part of his stand-up comedy act.

Sandler strums a tune on a *Saturday Night Live* "Weekend Update" segment.

UPDATE WEEKEND UPD

## Crazy for Candy

Some of Adam's best bits on *Saturday Night Live* seemed like they could have been made up by middle-school kids. On Halloween, for example, he gave costume advice on "Weekend Update." You don't need a fancy costume to get candy, he said. For example, you could scare people into giving you candy by dressing up as Crazy Sneaker Hand (he put a sneaker on his hand). Or, you could be Crazy Newspaper Face (he stuffed a newspaper in his shirt so it looked like he had a newspaper for a head). A huge laugh came when Adam ducked down under the "Weekend Update" desk. "I'm Crazy Guy Under the Desk!" he shouted. "Just 'cause you can't see me don't mean I don't want candy. Just leave the candy on the desk. I am warning you, do not come down here. Did I mention I was ... crazy?"

For this "Gap Girls" bit on *SNL*, David Spade (left), Chris Farley (right), and Adam all dressed in women's clothing.

He went to New York University (NYU) but spent little time on his studies. Instead, he hung out with his friends. He also worked on his stand-up act at comedy clubs in New York City.

## TV Breakout

In 1987, Adam got his first TV break — a small part on *The Cosby Show*. He was only twenty-one years old. His kind of comedy also appealed to MTV. He played "Stud Boy" on MTV's quiz show *Remote Control*.

Adam appeared in his first movie in 1989. The film was a low-budget quickie called *Going Overboard*. Around this time, he settled in Los Angeles. He started making the rounds of L.A.'s comedy clubs. At one club, Dennis Miller caught his act. Miller had become famous doing fake news on *Saturday Night Live*, or *SNL*.

Miller put in a good word with Lorne Michaels, the producer of *SNL*. Michaels then hired Adam as a comedy writer for the series. A year later, Sandler became a full-time member of the Not Ready for Prime Time Players.

## Fact File

*Saturday Night Live* is the longest-running comedy series in American TV history. It started in 1975 and is still going strong.

On *SNL*, Adam found a perfect place for his shtick. He was Canteen Boy, an overgrown kid in a Boy Scout outfit. He was Opera Man, who sang the week's news in a silly Italian accent. He was Cajun Man, answering every question with a single word that rhymed with SHUN. "How's your love life?" Kevin Nealon would ask. "Rejec-SHUN," Cajun Man would answer.

Adam with *SNL* cast members in the early 1990s. His friends on the show included Chris Farley (front row, left), Chris Rock (far left), and Rob Schneider (second row, right).

# King of Comedy

By 1993, Adam had a large following on *Saturday Night Live*. He began looking for new worlds to conquer.

His first step was to put out a comedy album, *They're All Gonna Laugh at You*. Like his later comedy CDs, it's a mixture of skits and songs. They show the raunchy side of Adam. Each of his comedy CDs has a Parental Advisory sticker.

Next, Adam looked to the big screen. He had a clear plan for success. Surround yourself with people you like and trust. (For Adam, these people were his old buddies from NYU.) Take a subject you know well. Keep the story simple. Do some of the gross bits and funny voices your fans like. Give your audience a feel-good ending.

In *Billy Madison* (1995), he plays a twenty-seven-year-old school dropout who bets his father he can finish all twelve grades in six

## Too Much Product?

Movies cost millions of dollars to make. Sometimes, moviemakers get help from big companies. The companies pay to have their products shown in a film. This practice is called product placement.

Roger Ebert is a well-known movie critic. He complained about product placement in Adam's movie *Happy Gilmore*. Ebert griped about the many plugs for Subway sandwich shops. He spotted a Subway sandwich eaten outside a store, a date in a Subway store, and a Subway soft drink container. He also noted a Subway ad starring Happy, a Subway T-shirt, and a Subway golf bag. "Halfway through the movie," Ebert wrote, "I didn't know what I wanted more: laughs, or mustard."

**Another product plug? Adam's T-shirt in *Happy Gilmore* delivers the message.**

months. In *Happy Gilmore* (1996), he's a lousy hockey player who learns how to control his anger and win at golf. In *Big Daddy* (1999), he's a slacker who learns how to be a good dad. In each movie, he starts out as a lovable loser and ends as an even more lovable winner.

## Winning More Fans

Adam continues to make these kinds of movies. Why not? His diehard fans love them. But he has also widened his appeal. He starred with Drew Barrymore in two successful romantic comedies, *The Wedding Singer* (1998) and *50 First Dates* (2004). He says it's fun working with Drew. "She's so relaxed, and she makes acting look so easy."

When Adam showed his softer side, the makers of serious films took notice. Paul Thomas Anderson cast him in the drama *Punch-Drunk Love* (2002). Another moviemaker, James L. Brooks, gave him a juicy part in *Spanglish* (2004). In each film, Adam has shown he can be likable and funny even without the usual Adam Sandler jokes.

## Fact File

Bill Murray, Eddie Murphy, and Mike Myers are *SNL* alumni who made hit movies. So is Rob Schneider, who is one of Adam's good friends.

## Movie Couples

Some screen couples have a special place in movie history. Fred Astaire and Ginger Rogers are a famous film couple. So are Spencer Tracy and Katharine Hepburn. Humphrey Bogart and Lauren Bacall are a famous pairing, too. Will Adam Sandler and Drew Barrymore take their places among these Hollywood legends? They'll need to make a few more movies together before we know for sure.

**Drew and Adam share a romantic moment in *50 First Dates*.**

# Twenty Million Dollar Man

# Chapter 5

Adam Sandler has many reasons to be happy. At twenty million dollars a movie, he's one of the best-paid actors in Hollywood. He writes and produces films for himself and his friends. He still hangs out with many of his old buddies from college and *SNL*. In June 2003, he married actress and model Jacqueline "Jackie" Titone.

When Adam was younger, his love life had more than a few setbacks. He told *E! Online* that his toughest breakup was in sixth grade. While he ate dinner with his parents, his girlfriend Kim called. She told him she was dumping him. He lied to his parents about why Kim had called. He "tried not to cry the whole dinner."

A girlfriend from his teen years told a

## Fact File

Adam Sandler has signed to appear in *Click*. In this romantic comedy, he discovers a special kind of remote control. It allows him to see both his future and his past. The film is expected to open in the summer of 2006.

## Fact File

Jackie Titone, shown here
with Adam on their wedding
day, has been in many of Adam's
recent movies. She had roles in
*Eight Crazy Nights* and *50 First Dates*.

## Big Laughs, Big Bucks

For most movie comedies, opening weekend is key. If a lot of people see the film that first weekend — and they like it — they'll spread the word. They'll tell their friends. Better still, they'll bring their friends to share the laughs again and again.

Adam gets paid $20 million a movie because his films "open big." An Adam Sandler comedy attracts large crowds even if the local newspaper gives it a bad review. *50 First Dates* opened on Valentine's Day weekend in 2004. The film earned almost $40 million that first weekend. The movie went on to make nearly $200 million around the world — and that's not counting DVD rentals and sales. Not a bad payday!

reporter that dating him "was like dating all three stooges at once." When they broke up, he "ran off laughing, crying, flapping his arms like a bird and hollering, 'She loves me! She loves me not!'"

Rumor has it that Adam came close to marrying Margaret Ruden in the mid-1990s. She worked in the cosmetics industry and met Adam after one of his shows. They were together for about six years until they broke up in 1995. After that breakup, Adam was linked to actress Alicia Silverstone.

Adam first met Jackie at a party in Los Angeles. By 1999, he was telling everybody he was in love. "I got hit hard," he said. Four years later, they were married.

Adam accepts a 2004 Kids' Choice Award from Queen Latifah (left) and Katie Thomas.

## Kids' Choice

Adam isn't the kind of actor who wins a lot of awards from movie critics. But he's won quite a few honors from the people who actually buy movie tickets and DVDs. He won Nickelodeon Kids' Choice Awards as Favorite Movie Actor in 1999, 2000, and 2003. In 2004, he won the Kids' Choice Wannabe Award, given to the famous person kids would most like to be. He earned a People's Choice Award in 2000, and he and Drew Barrymore won the award for favorite on-screen couple in 2005. Teen Choice Awards went to Adam four straight years, from 2001 to 2004. Adam was probably much less thrilled with another award he received for 1999. For his performance in *Big Daddy*, he won the Golden Raspberry — the Razzie — for Worst Actor.

## Familiar Faces

Adam likes to work with familiar faces. Many of his buddies were on the set for the 2005 film *The Longest Yard*. The movie is a remake of a Hollywood classic that came out in 1974. Adam plays a former football star who lands in jail. He has to put together a team of convicts to play against a team of prison guards.

Chris Rock co-stars in the film. He and Adam worked together on *Saturday Night Live* in the early 1990s. Peter Segal directed the film. He was Adam's director for *Anger Management* and *50 First Dates*. Burt Reynolds is another familiar face in the movie. He starred in the 1974 version of *The Longest Yard*.

The wedding took place in Malibu, California, on a cliff overlooking the ocean. It was a formal affair. But Adam made sure there were some comic touches. His bulldog, Meatball, wore a black dinner jacket and a white yarmulke — just like Adam. Matzoball was there, too. This bulldog was a gift to Adam from Jackie.

The newlyweds made sure nobody left the wedding hungry. Every guest was given a box of Krispy Kreme donuts. Each box had a picture of Meatball and Matzoball, along with these words: "Eat your donuts before we do."

**Everyone wore formal clothes to Adam and Jackie's wedding — including Adam's bulldog, Meatball.**

28

# Time Line

**1966**    Adam Richard Sandler is born on September 9 in Brooklyn, New York.

**1987**    Lands his first TV role, on *The Cosby Show*.

**1991**    Becomes a regular on *Saturday Night Live*.

**1993**    Releases his first comedy album, *They're All Gonna Laugh at You*.

**1995**    Stars in the film *Billy Madison*.

**1998**    Co-stars with Drew Barrymore in *The Wedding Singer*.

**2002**    Has his first role in a serious drama, *Punch-Drunk Love*.

**2003**    Marries Jackie Titone.

**2004**    Co-stars with Drew Barrymore in their second hit film, *50 First Dates*.

**2005**    Stars with Chris Rock in the film *The Longest Yard*.

# Glossary

**alumni** — former members.

**cosmetics** — materials used to make a person more attractive, such as lipstick or face powder.

**Hanukkah** — a Jewish holiday that usually begins in December and lasts for eight days. It is also spelled Chanukah.

**movie critics** — people who make their living by giving their opinions about movies.

**Parental Advisory sticker** — a warning label to parents. It tells them that the language or subject matter of a CD may not be suitable for children.

**prime time** — the part of the evening when most people watch television.

**producer** — someone who raises the money and hires the people for a TV series or a movie.

**shtick** — Yiddish for "piece" or "prank," a kind of comedy that depends on a few basic gags and gimmicks.

**underestimated** — underrated or taken for granted.

**yarmulke** — a Jewish skullcap, usually worn for religious purposes.

**Yiddish** — a language spoken by some Jews, especially Jews from Eastern Europe. Many Yiddish words have become part of the English language.

# To Find Out More

**Books**

*Adam Sandler.* People in the News (series).
　Dwayne Epstein (Lucent Books)

*Funny Bones: Comedy Games and Activities for Kids.*
　Lisa Bany-Winters (Chicago Review Press)

*The Hanukkah Story.* Holiday Stories (series).
　Anita Ganeri (Smart Apple Media)


**Videos**

*50 First Dates* (Columbia Tristar) PG-13

*Saturday Night Live: The Best of Adam Sandler*
　(Lions Gate) TV-14

*The Waterboy* (Touchstone) PG-13

*The Wedding Singer* (New Line) PG-13


**Web Sites**

Official Adam Sandler Web Site
*www.adamsandler.com*
News about Adam, as well as videos and cartoons

The Internet Movie Database
*www.imdb.com*
Facts about movies and the people who make them

# Index

## About the Author

Geoffrey M. Horn has been a fan of music, movies, and sports for as long as he can remember. He has written more than a dozen books for young people and adults, along with hundreds of articles on many different subjects. He lives in southwestern Virginia, in the foothills of the Blue Ridge Mountains, with his wife, their collie, and four cats. He dedicates this book to class clowns everywhere (he was one of them).